Watch Your Wealth

Torah Guidelines
for Financial Success

Watch Your Wealth

Torah Guidelines

for Financial Success

TARGUM/FELDHEIM

First published 2001/5761

Copyright © 2001 by Moshe Goldberger

P.O. Box 82

Staten Island, N.Y. 10309

Tel. 718-948-2548

ISBN: 1-56871-168-9

Published by: **Targum Press Inc.**

22700 W. Eleven Mile Rd.

Southfield, Mich. 48034

targum@netvision.net.il

Fax: 888-298-9992

Distributed by: **Feldheim Publishers**

200 Airport Executive Park

Nanuet, N.Y. 10954

www.feldheim.com

Printed in Israel

This publication has been dedicated

by

Hershey and Raisy Friedman

of Montreal, Canada

With thanks to:
Rabbi Eliezer Gevirtz
Rabbi Menachem Goldman
Rabbi Mordechai Gelber
Yitzchok E. Gold
Binyamin Siegel
Charles S. Mamiye
Jonathan Friedman
Dr. F. Glatter
and others

Contents

MONEY LESSONS FROM *MISHLEI* 11

    Introduction · · · · · · · · · · · · · · · · · 13

    Two Secrets · · · · · · · · · · · · · · · · · 15

    The Leaf Principle · · · · · · · · · · · · · 18

    Value Control · · · · · · · · · · · · · · · · 22

    The Crown of the Wise · · · · · · · · · · · 25

    Giving to Receive · · · · · · · · · · · · · 28

    Luxury or Necessity? · · · · · · · · · · · · 30

    What Is Precious? · · · · · · · · · · · · · 33

    Humility and Wealth · · · · · · · · · · · 36

    Use Your Wisdom · · · · · · · · · · · · · 38

    Benefits of Being Fearful · · · · · · · · · · 40

MONEY LESSONS FROM *PIRKEI AVOS* 43

    Introduction · · · · · · · · · · · · · · · · · 45

    His Money · · · · · · · · · · · · · · · · · · 46

    Your Responsibility · · · · · · · · · · · · · 48

    Behind a Savings Plan · · · · · · · · · · · 51

    Doing His Will · · · · · · · · · · · · · · · 54

    Directing Your Thoughts · · · · · · · · · · 56

    Positive Thoughts · · · · · · · · · · · · · 59

    Words and Action · · · · · · · · · · · · · 61

Priorities · · · · · · · · · · · · · · 63

Proper Use of Wealth · · · · · · · · · 66

Three Foundations · · · · · · · · · · 68

BUSINESS LESSONS 71

Introduction · · · · · · · · · · · · · 73

Wide Open · · · · · · · · · · · · · · 75

Be Sincere · · · · · · · · · · · · · · 78

Promote Your Message · · · · · · · · · 80

Six Super Seconds · · · · · · · · · 83

Loving Others · · · · · · · · · · · · 85

Learning from Others · · · · · · · · · 87

Say a Little · · · · · · · · · · · · · 89

Who to Blame · · · · · · · · · · · · 91

Cherishing Your Friend's Money · · · · · 93

Wealth Insurance · · · · · · · · · · · 95

THE BENEFITS OF GIVING *MA'ASER* 97

Introduction · · · · · · · · · · · · · 99

Benefits of Giving · · · · · · · · · 102

Keep Growing · · · · · · · · · · · 104

Comparison Motivation · · · · · · · · 106

Training Oneself · · · · · · · · · · 108

Give from What You Have · · · · · · · 110

Why We Give · · · · · · · · · · · 111

Unlimited Giving · · · · · · · · · · 113

Giving Is Living · · · · · · · · · · · 114

THE *ALEF-BEIS* OF MAKING MONEY
THE TORAH WAY 117

Part I

Money Lessons
from Mishlei

Introduction

If you seek it like silver and search for it as for hidden treasures, you will understand the fear of Hashem and find knowledge.
(*Mishlei* 2:4)

People desire wealth. They yearn for acquisition, never satisfied with what they have. But this yearning is not limited to the desire for physical possessions. Our inner souls yearn for the true wealth of Torah knowledge and mitzvah acquisitions that we will take with us for eternity.

Since we are human, we need both money and Torah to sustain us (see *Avos* 3:12). What determines how we make money? How are we supposed to spend what we earn? What will money do for us? The answers to these questions, and more, come from the Torah and the Sages who teach its wisdom.

As we study the sources on how to become materially wealthy and how to deal with wealth, we should keep in mind that they can all be understood on a deeper level, namely, how to acquire spiritual wealth. Although this is not dealt with in this work, a Torah Jew must realize that money is a gift from Hashem, to be used for the fulfillment of mitzvos.

Every one of us needs money to perform the mitzvos of providing for ourselves and for our families, paying off our debts, paying for our children's Torah education, succeeding in Torah, and doing acts of kindness.

At the same time, however, we must not ignore or forget about the true wealth we possess: health, family, friends, a warm home. While we remind ourselves of Hashem's gifts to us, we can also pursue material riches.

Lesson One

Two Secrets

The hand of the diligent will become wealthy.
(*Mishlei* 10:4)

It is Hashem's blessing that makes one wealthy.
(*Mishlei* 10:22)

The same chapter of Mishlei teaches that both the diligent hand and Hashem's blessing will lead to wealth. Both principles are essential. In order to become wealthy, a person needs to

1. Work diligently with integrity, and

2. Pray to the Master of all wealth.

Of these two verses, the wording of the second one is more emphatic, implying that Hashem's blessing is the true cause of all wealth. Hashem is the source of all goodness. He provides everything and He gives prosperity to those whom He decides to benefit. However, one of His considerations is how much effort we put in.

Regarding the diligence required, we have another verse which instructs us, "Do not overexert yourself to become wealthy" (*Mishlei* 23:4). Overexertion shows that you think it is in your hands to produce. This is a false assumption, for the true key is Heavenly assistance. You must invest adequate effort, but Hashem is the one who decides how much wealth to bestow upon you.

> *Hashem puts people to death and He brings them to life.... Hashem makes them poor and wealthy; He lowers them, and He raises them up.*
> (*Shmuel* I, 2:6–7)

How does Hashem choose who gets what, how much, and when? We have a number of hints from the Torah — insights into Hashem's system for determining whom He causes to prosper.

The Gemara (*Nidah* 70b) asks outright: "What can a person do to become wealthy?" (This follows the instructions of what to do to become wise, which is the first priority. See the Gemara there for more insight.)

The Gemara answers:

1. Conduct your business with integrity, and

2. Pray for mercy from the Owner of all wealth.

In general, Hashem chooses to prosper the person who fulfills the mitzvah of emulating His ways. Hashem created the world with kindness and His ways of dealing with it are all kindness. To emulate Him, we have to treat others kindly in our business or occupation. If we do this, keeping in mind that it is our way of serving Hashem, we will merit more funds from Hashem, so that we can continue treating others kindly in this position.

Included in diligence is perseverance. Hashem has a way of testing people to see if they can be trusted to serve as His financial agents in this world. Disappointments have to be accepted gracefully. "A tzaddik may fall seven times, yet he rises" (*Mishlei* 24:16).

There are three vital methods of operation that should never be forgotten: persistence, patience, and prayer. Persist in your efforts patiently, with prayer.

The Leaf Principle

*One who trusts in his wealth will fall, but the
tzaddikim will flourish like leaves.*
(*Mishlei* 11:28)

The Vilna Gaon interprets the second half of this
verse to mean, "The tzaddikim who consider
their wealth like leaves will succeed." He explains:
Leaves are not the main component of a tree. If you
consider your money the most important thing in
your life and trust in it; you may find that it will dis-
appear. Just as coins are designed like wheels, which
can roll away from you (*Shabbos* 151b), bills are like
leaves, which can easily blow away in the wind.

A wise person considers money like leaves. Although leaves are very useful, providing protection
for the fruit and shade for people, as well as filling
the air with oxygen, there is also a time when they
fall down.

Money can provide us with many benefits, by
enabling us to buy all our daily needs and luxuries,

too. We appreciate the physical benefits of money, but we have to be cautious with our attitude toward it, because it demonstrates who we are — by our thoughts, words, and actions. Not only are we affected by our attitude toward money, but it also resonates and affects others.

Do we work to make money, or do we work because we are serving Hashem? Is our primary goal in life merely to succeed at our career and enjoy the benefits of hard work, or do we also apply ourselves to our jobs because we want to please Hashem?

All your deeds should be for the sake of Heaven.
(*Avos* 2:17)

If there is no sustenance, there is no Torah.
(Ibid. 3:21)

A person can transform his work hours into a Torah-sustaining session if he practices focusing and directing his thoughts and speech properly.

Hashem, who makes the leaves grow, provides sustenance for all of mankind. As we say three times a day in *Ashrei*, "You open Your hand and satiate the desires of all the living" (*Tehillim* 145:16). We have to recognize that Hashem's hand is sending us our paycheck or our clients, and relate to Him with gratitude and submission.

One way to do this would be to train ourselves to look at the phrase "In G-d we trust" at least once a day when handling money. As you do this, tell yourself, "Don't trust in the money itself." Money is useful, but it does not last very long in the final scheme of things. Our purpose in this world is not to make money, but rather to learn Torah and do mitzvos.

When you stop worshiping money, you will be surprised to discover that you may begin to make more of it than before, as the Vilna Gaon teaches: Those who consider their wealth like leaves will succeed.

We must learn to bend with the wind, as leaves do. Don't stiffen up when dealing with competition or opposition. Submit to Hashem's control. He is always trying to help you. Even when you think that you are losing a great job or business opportunity, realize that it is for the best; Hashem has the complete picture in mind. "Everything is in Hashem's hands" (*Berachos* 33b). "This, too, is for your benefit" (*Taanis* 21a).

When we lose money periodically, we can use it as an opportunity to remind ourselves not to focus so much on money. Focus instead on the tree — i.e., the Source of the leaves, Hashem, who is the Source of all wealth. Be flexible and keep praying to Hashem with the realization that He sends you all that you need. You can be wealthier — in deeds as well as in money — if you avoid the error of thinking that money solves problems. Trust in Hashem, who solves problems and produces all the money we need.

Daily Checklist:

❖ Upgrade your diligence.

❖ Increase your prayer for Hashem's blessing.

❖ Look at some leaves and think of *Mishlei* 11:28.

Value Control

One who disdains a thing will suffer from it.
(*Mishlei* 13:13)

The Mishnah teaches, "Do not be disdainful of anything...for everything has its place" (*Avos* 4:3).

When you neglect your finances, they tend to dwindle. When you treat them with respect, Hashem causes your endeavors to prosper and grow on your behalf. Bills should be paid in a timely fashion and in a responsible way. "Paying one's debts is a mitzvah" (*Kesubos* 86a).

You have to be organized to pay your debts and to save money. When you begin to pay attention to doing things correctly, Hashem makes you aware of ideas that will aid you and improve the quality of your work.

When your belongings are in a clutter, you cannot properly appreciate each item's individual benefits. If you organize yourself and focus better, you will be able to enjoy each item that you have, and you will also receive more from Hashem.

Hashem has plenty of money, and He loves you greatly. He observes the way you treat the money He has given you, and He measures your future income accordingly. If you show that you appreciate what He has given you until now, you will be blessed with more.

Train yourself to appreciate the things you already have by asking:

❖ Do I know what I have and where everything is?

❖ Do I own things I don't want or need?

❖ Do I value that which I own?

Your possessions represent who you are, how you define yourself, your tastes, and your values. The Chafetz Chaim was said to have an accounting of the hours he could have used for learning more Torah, but, instead, used to work in order to pay for the meager possessions that he owned.

Think about the value of what you own and how it represents who you are. If you place too much value on material objects, you are forgetting that this world is only temporary; nothing here lasts forever. Hashem will eventually take and not give if you tend to value money, expensive furnishings, clothing, or fancy electronic equipment over Torah and mitzvos.

It is also important to properly appreciate what

you have and use it in the appropriate way.

Just as one who undervalues something will suffer (see above, *Mishlei* 13:13), a person who undervalues his job skills and the services he provides will also suffer. Although the Torah expects us to be humble, we must still know our own worth. For example, if you don't charge at least the going rate for your services because you undervalue what you do, others will also undervalue who you are and what you stand for! In addition to losing out monetarily, you will lose out socially and emotionally.

The Crown of the Wise

Wealth is a crown of the wise.
(*Mishlei* 14:24)

Metzudas David explains that a wise person utilizes his wealth to increase his generosity and enhance his glory in many ways. A fool, on the other hand, demonstrates his foolishness by how he misuses his wealth.

Wealth is a tool that can be used to promote truth, justice, and Torah. It can serve as a crown to elevate a sage, enhancing his stature in the eyes of others. The Gemara lists wealth as one of many things that are beneficial in limited amounts, but harmful in excess (*Gittin* 70a). How do you gauge how much is too much? Rashi explains that wealth is proper as long as it does not detract from the person's spiritual growth and Torah study, and it does not lead to arrogance.

Why is the purchase price of wisdom in the hand
of a fool if he has no sense?
(*Mishlei* 17:16)

Money is not the key to happiness nor the key to wisdom. It can merely assist a wise person in achieving his goals.

The Gemara teaches that a person should always avoid guaranteeing a loan (*Yevamos* 109a). Why? Rabbeinu Yonah explains: First, because guaranteeing a loan usually leads to quarrels, and second, because one is obligated to protect his assets and avoid such risks.

It is certainly a mitzvah to lend money and to help someone else obtain a loan by serving as the guarantor. However, one should only guarantee a loan if he is ready to pay the amount if it will be necessary. Avoid signing for a loan if you cannot pay up.

We have to be cautious and consider how to utilize wealth in positive ways, not in ways that might cause harm to others or to ourselves.

Wealth is only a crown if our minds are controlling our fears and our greed. Without proper control over your inclination to buy more and more or over your fears that you will lose your money, you may become a foolish rich person, who will never be truly satisfied with what he has (see *Avos* 4:1). Choose your thoughts and your attitude to money instead of reacting to your emotions. When you do so, you will be utilizing and developing your crown. Don't let money or bills cloud your clear thinking or lead you away from the path of Torah.

When you use your brain properly, your mind will show you ways of making money that others don't notice. Hashem will open your mind to opportunities that are in easy reach.

Wisdom is before an understanding person [the solution is right before him], but a fool looks to the ends of the earth.
(*Mishlei* 17:24)

Giving to Receive

*A person's giving opens the way for him and
brings him before great men.*
(*Mishlei* 18:16)

The Vilna Gaon connects this *pasuk* to "Give a
tenth [of your money] to charity so that you will
become wealthy" (*Taanis* 9a). A person who is generous will develop many relationships that will help
him prosper. This is a built-in benefit provided by
Hashem, a dividend for good deeds.

In addition, Hashem is watching us to see how
we utilize the funds He provides us with. When He
sees us using the funds wisely and sharing with others, He provides us with more.

This brings us to one of Shlomo HaMelech's
most important prayers to Hashem:

Poverty and wealth do not give me.
(*Mishlei* 30:8)

The proper financial balance is something we

have to keep praying to Hashem for. If you have too much and you feel that you don't deserve it, or if you have less than enough and feel you deserve more, turn to Hashem for help. We have to properly utilize all of the funds that Hashem provides us with.

There is only one way to become wealthy: to merit receiving money from the Creator of all wealth. Why would Hashem desire to give you wealth? Do you know how to utilize it? Will you be dedicating it for *tikun ha'olam* (improving the world)?

You can accomplish tremendous good if you decide to do just that — improve the world. Hashem is looking for people who choose to be givers. He gives to them because they give to others.

If you claim you want to be rich in order to help others yet you rarely give money to *tzedakah*, who are you trying to fool? Hashem wants you to start taking positive action, slowly, one step at a time. He will work with you, but you have to do your part.

Luxury or Necessity?

*One who loves wine and oil [i.e., luxuries] will
not become wealthy.*
(*Mishlei* 21:17)

One who is enslaved by the desire for instant gratification will not have the patience or commitment necessary for developing his finances. There is a trick question used to point out this lesson: If someone would offer you a choice of either $1,000 a day for thirty days or thirty days of money, beginning with a penny on the first day and doubling the amount each day after that, which would you choose?

The first choice gets you an easy $30,000. The second choice, on the other hand, starts with only a small amount, but it will eventually yield millions of dollars. It takes effort to do this calculation, and people tend to be reluctant to put in effort when they feel there is an easy way out. This, however, is not the purpose of life. "Man was created for toil" (*Iyov* 5:7). The Mishnah says, "Love work" (*Avos* 1:10). It does not say, "Love money," but rather, love the work.

As Yaakov Avinu was preparing to meet his brother Eisav after staying with Lavan for twenty years, he retraced his steps to retrieve some small containers (even though he was by then quite wealthy). Why did he bother? He valued them for they represented the honest efforts he had made to acquire them in the first place. (See *Bereishis* 32:25.)

The words quoted at the beginning of this lesson are the second half of a verse in *Mishlei*. The verse in its entirety says: "A person who loves to have a good time will be lacking; one who loves wine and oil will not become wealthy."

We have to learn to make the right choices. If we keep indulging in luxuries, we will begin to think that they are necessities and our cost of living will go up. We can lose a lot this way — an unnecessary pleasure now can cause a loss of greater pleasures tomorrow.

You can change your course and become rich if you save part of your money or invest it instead of spending. You can make every dollar count. Every financial choice will make a difference — you just need to eliminate bad habits that cause your money to evaporate.

You can find more money by examining your expenses, distinguishing between necessity and luxury, trimming your spending, and training yourself to value money over unnecessary items.

Daily Checklist:

❖ How can I organize myself better?

❖ Do I allow my wealth to control me?

❖ How can I give more and become more wealthy?

❖ Do I need to earn more? Why?

What Is Precious?

Costly items and oil are stored in a wise person's home; a fool swallows up [his assets].
(*Mishlei* 21:20)

What are the acquisitions we want most in life? The basic, fundamental answer is food, clothing, and money. But stop and ask yourself, Do I really need money? If you had everything that money could buy, you would not actually need any money at all.

Thus, this verse does not say, "A wise person saves money." Rather, it says, "Costly items and oil [i.e., precious items] are stored in a wise person's house."

We need to analyze what we are saving and why. People often buy unnecessary items which quickly lose their value. Instead of doing this, we should save money so that we will be able to buy that which we may need in the future.

The Torah instructs us, when dealing with

money, to "Wrap the money in your hand" (*Devarim* 14:25). This is explained by the Gemara (*Bava Metzia* 42a and *Rashi*) to mean: "A person should always keep his money readily available...and he should divide it into three parts:

"1. One third [invested] in real estate [which is more secure],

"2. One third in merchandise [which yields greater profits], and

"3. One third in liquid assets [in order to be able to benefit from sudden opportunities]."

We have to learn to value our money so that we do not part with it so freely. Saving and investing, the Gemara teaches, are very important. Of course, we should never spend money we don't even have yet by buying things on credit.

The Gemara uses strong language to impress upon us the proper use and value of money: "A righteous person cherishes his money more than his body" (*Chullin* 91a).

What are you living for? None of us knows how much time he has left in this world. Your job is to utilize your money to serve Hashem. To have millions of dollars in the bank without a plan or purpose for them is not an objective of life. What is it there for? You have been put here to do Hashem's will, and you must serve Hashem by doing that which He created you for. Not just saving money, but utilizing it as the Torah dictates.

Ask yourself:

❖ When was the last time I balanced my portfolio with the Torah's guidelines?

Humility and Wealth

Humility leads to wealth.
(*Mishlei* 22:4)

Hashem is eager to help His people. But if we do not appreciate His help, if we take credit for ourselves, we may find ourselves with nothing. Hashem does not want to waste His bounty on those who are ungrateful.

Who is wise? He who sees the future.
(*Avos* 4:1)

One who puts today's desires before tomorrow's needs is usually one whose ego is inflated. A humble person is more thoughtful and more practical. He or she keeps tomorrow in mind today. A humble person will save money.

A humble person will also desire to be rich. Why? Because he understands that everything is in Hashem's hands. Hashem is the only One who makes people wealthy. He created each one of us with unlimited greatness, to the extent that we are obligated to declare: "Because of me, Hashem created the universe" (*Sanhedrin* 37a).

When a person is a humble servant of the Owner of all wealth, he will dedicate himself to utilizing wealth properly. Avraham, Yitzchak, and Yaakov Avinu, Yosef HaTzaddik, Moshe Rabbeinu, David, and Shlomo HaMelech were all very humble and very wealthy. In addition, the Gemara (*Nedarim* 38a) lists wealth as one of the prerequisites for a person to become a prophet.

To really make money, you need to sober up and realize that a Jew should not make money for a living. He does it to live a life of Torah and serve Hashem and people. Those who make money for a living are tempted, at times, to compromise on their principles. But if you make money to live a Torah life, you will work hard, with honesty, integrity, and humility, to do what Hashem requires of you. Then success is guaranteed!

Lesson Nine

Use Your Wisdom

With wisdom, one's rooms will be filled with all kinds of precious and pleasant wealth.
(Mishlei 24:4)

Your success or failure in financial matters greatly depends on your thoughts. "Every person who has wisdom will eventually become wealthy" (*Sanhedrin* 92a). Maharsha on this *gemara* explains: A person who has Torah wisdom knows that in order to achieve wealth he must also invest great effort in praying for mercy from the Owner of all wealth.

To make more money and to utilize money wisely, we need to learn to develop our wisdom more. We need the right attitudes to get the right results. By learning to think clearly and by filling our minds and hearts with Torah wisdom, we will be able to manage our finances in a clear-headed way.

When the Torah teaches the need to work for a living, it says: "By the sweat of your brow you will eat bread" (*Bereishis* 3:17). Rabbi Shamshon Refael

Hirsch points out that it does not say, "By the sweat of your *hands*." Hashem wants us to use our minds to develop ways to earn money.

The Gemara teaches that a person should train for a profession that is "clean and light" (*Kiddushin* 82a). This requires learning and preparation — how else will one know if he is choosing an appropriate profession? Without studying and applying the Torah sources, we will not know how to handle the monetary challenges of life.

Lesson Ten

Benefits of Being Fearful

Fortunate is the person who is constantly afraid.
(*Mishlei* 28:14)

Many people are afraid that they won't be able to pay their bills, that they will lose their jobs, and that they won't be able to support their families. These fears are good as long as they motivate us to recognize that we need Hashem's help in everything that we do. Daven to Him, because prayer is most essential to becoming wealthy, as the Talmud teaches (*Nidah* 70b).

We have to learn to confront our fears and replace them with encouraging and helpful Torah thoughts. Never allow your fear to paralyze you.

Train yourself to constantly say and think: "Hashem is my Shepherd; I will not be lacking.... I will not fear evil, for You [Hashem] are with me..." (*Tehillim* 23:1, 3). You will have enough money if you trust in Hashem.

You can review this lesson every day before going to work (or looking for work, if that is the case), and then put it in your own words. If you have to earn $5,000 a month, for example, to cover your family's budget, say to yourself: "I will be able to earn at least five thousand dollars a month with Hashem's help."

Say it ten times a day, and you will see that it will become part of your regular thinking pattern, and it will come true. Whenever you start to worry or become anxious, repeat the above verses from *Tehillim* 23 again and again.

We are not like Eisav, who said, "I have much" (*Bereishis* 33:9). Rather, we follow Yaakov Avinu, who said, "Hashem was gracious to me and I have everything" (ibid., 11).

Instead of being afraid to deal with your financial needs, be afraid of failing to fulfill your monetary obligations to Hashem and to people. If you were never afraid, you would not be motivated to daven properly.

Don't drive yourself crazy worrying about what might go wrong; focus, instead, on what you desire to go right. Believe in Hashem and trust His assurances. Do your part every day, even if you are afraid you won't succeed, because Hashem will come through, He always does. In actuality, Hashem is only waiting for you to come through — His response is immediate.

Part II

Money Lessons from

Pirkei Avos

Introduction

Everything we do in this world has or should have a purpose. Earning money and spending it are not neutral acts. Rather, there are many mitzvos and *aveiros* that relate to them, which we must acknowledge.

Everything in this world is a challenge for us. Money is an especially tricky challenge, as we will learn. But we cannot avoid dealing with it. "If there is no sustenance, there is no Torah" (*Avos* 3:21).

Four activities require constant strengthening: Torah, good deeds, prayer, and earning a livelihood.
(*Berachos* 32b, according to *Rashi*)

Why is earning a living counted as one of the four activities that require *chizuk*? Rabbi Isaac Sher, zt"l, explains this is because it is the means through which one supports his Torah and *chesed* activities.

Lesson One

His Money

*Give [Hashem] of His, for you and all that is
yours are actually His.*
(*Avos* 3:8)

This is a most basic, essential Torah principle.

No matter what you give Hashem, it will never be something that He did not give you first. Your labor results from the body and energy that He provides. Your mind is a gift from Him to you. The ideas you ponder come from Him, and we are commanded, "Remember Hashem, your G-d, who provides you with the power to achieve" (*Devarim* 8:18). *Targum Onkelos* translates this verse: "He gives you the insights to buy assets."

The Gemara teaches that a person should give ten percent of his earnings to charity in order to become wealthy (*Taanis* 9a). When you give *tzedakah*, however, you must understand that this blessing may not come to fruition if you think that you are doing Hashem a "favor" by giving the poor some of your money. Rather, you must realize that you are only giving Hashem some of His own. It is all His! He merely appoints us as guardians to distribute the money and utilize it for various causes.

Imagine yourself as a bank teller who works for the Owner of all banks, Hashem Yisbarach. It should not be at all painful for you to give away a million dollars to charity, if you have earned ten million. It is only a small part of that which Hashem has given you. When He sees you performing your duty, He will provide you with more wealth to distribute for Him.

Your Responsibility

In *Avos* 2:13, five Sages teach us keys to success. One of the five, Rabbi Shimon, states that the best method to insure one's success is to always look ahead. Several mishnayos later, we read:

> *Rabbi Shimon says: Be exceedingly careful in Krias Shema and in prayer. When you pray, do not make your prayer a fixed routine, but rather [pray for] mercy and supplication before Hashem.... And do not consider yourself wicked.*
>
> (*Avos* 2:18)

What is the connection between these three teachings of Rabbi Shimon?

Looking to the future is a Torah obligation that helps a person achieve every form of perfection.

> *Who is wise? He who sees the future.*
>
> (*Avos* 4:1)

A prudent person sees harm and protects himself;

a fool keeps going and suffers.
(*Mishlei* 22:5)

We can train ourselves to practice foresight and thus avoid many problems in life. Saving money, according to Torah guidelines, is a method of foreseeing and preparing for the future.

With this in mind, let us return to Rabbi Shimon's next teachings. There are many thoughts that accompany us throughout the day. However, we should try to concentrate on trusting Hashem, who is always in control. He provides for us, yet He requires us to make efforts to make money and take care of it. When we recite *krias Shema*, as Rabbi Shimon teaches, we should focus on recognizing that Hashem is always in complete control, and He is always there for us. We should also focus on loving Him with our whole heart, our soul, and our finances and dedicate ourselves to utilizing our assets according to His dictates.

Second, when we pray, we should realize that we need Hashem's help for every endeavor, and we hope He will bless our efforts and make us prosperous.

Third, we must focus on self-esteem. Don't allow yourself to become discouraged or think that Hashem does not desire to help you. He cares for you, He knows all your difficulties, and He is waiting eagerly to assist you more when you pray for His assistance.

By doing our part in prayer, Torah study, and efforts for *parnassah*, we become more worthy of Hashem's intervention on our behalf.

Behind a Savings Plan

Who is strong? He who conquers his evil inclina-
tion.... Who is wealthy? He who is happy with
his portion.
(*Avos* 4:1)

Saving one third of one's earnings (see above, p.34) will help a person work on his self-discipline. Putting money away for later use is a discipline: It indicates the ability to say, "No, not now" to oneself, and thereby develops one's strength to have long-term success in life.

In addition, when a person has a savings program, he will find many opportunities to focus on the mishnah's definition of wealth, to be "happy with one's portion." When you save, your spending money is limited, but you will gain in the long run by having what you need when you really need it.

A savings program enables a person to appreciate the bounty that Hashem provides for him or her. Just as Hashem wants us to eat and yet know that it is not the food that enables us to live — only His decree (see *Devarim* 8:3) — so, too, He wants us to save money and yet realize that He is the One who prospers our efforts.

Having money in the bank can help a person feel happy and self-confident, rather than nervous and anxious. However, this self-confidence can lead to the great problem of forgetting Hashem and thinking, "My power and might have made for me this wealth" (*Devarim* 8:10). Therefore, you must continuously remind yourself that it is Hashem who gives you the power to acquire and to save wealth.

What about *tzedakah*? Should one give all of his or her extra money away to *tzedakah*? No. The Gemara teaches, "One should not give away more than a fifth [of his earnings], so that he does not become dependent on others" (*Kesubos* 50a). We are obligated to be concerned not to become dependent on others. (There are five exceptions to this rule, as the Chafetz Chaim teaches in *Ahavas Chesed*, section 2, ch. 20).

We have to balance caring and providing for ourselves with realizing that we can do nothing without Hashem's help.

Money can solve many problems, providing us with extra time, peace of mind, and opportunities to be generous with charity. The more money we have, the more grateful we ought to be to Hashem for His bounty.

Is money "the root that leads to all evil," or is the lack of money a cause of evil? The answer is that there are Talmudic sources that support both sides, because whether a person has money or doesn't have it, he is being challenged by Hashem to see how he will deal with his situation in a Torah manner.

Lesson Four

Doing His Will

*Make His [Hashem's] will as your own, so that
He will make your will His. Cancel your will for
the sake of His will, so that He will cancel the
will of others for you.*
(*Avos* 2:4)

D o you want to make more money? Do you want
people to agree to do business with you and customers and clients to seek your services? Hashem
will help make it happen if you work with Him.

Twice a day, in Shema, we recite, "Love
Hashem, your G-d, with all your heart, all your soul,
and all your resources" (*Devarim* 6:5).

The word "resources" in Hebrew is "*me'odecha*,"
which literally means "very much." *Me'odecha* includes your strength, abilities, property, time, energy, and more. Everything we have is from
Hashem, and thus the principle of gratitude obli-
gates us to use our assets for the sake of Hashem.

As we work to earn money, we need to think

about working the way the Torah teaches us to work. Do you always show up for appointments on time? That is a Torah principle of the highest order. Do you pay attention and listen to others? Do you work with loyalty and treat others with respect? Do you do your best, or do you try to fool people?

Hashem gave you unique talents. Do you utilize them fully?

There are many parts to "doing His will." It is not always easy, but extremely worthwhile!

The Rambam ends the laws of *Sechirus* (earning a living) by teaching that the obligation of an employee is to work with all of his energy for his employer. This will lead to great wealth, the Rambam concludes, as we see from the results of Yaakov Avinu's work program (*Bereishis* 30:31–43).

Lesson Five

Directing Your Thoughts

Do not consider yourself wicked.
(*Avos* 2:18)

When a person thinks he is wicked, he behaves this way, too, and the situation turns from bad to worse. We must learn to steer away from negative thoughts and replace them with positive ones. Do Hashem's will, and think about things He desires you to think about.

Never think that you won't make it. Why shouldn't you? Hashem can help you succeed. He is All-powerful and the *Ba'al Rachamim* (source of all mercy). Think positive. With strong, positive thoughts and Hashem's help, you can lead a fulfilling life, full of achievements.

In the Shema, we are instructed to place the words of the Torah in our minds and have them accompany us everywhere. "When you sit in your home, when you travel on the road, before you fall asleep, and as soon as you arise" (*Devarim* 6:8). One should always be thinking or discussing positive Torah thoughts.

You can choose to think positive, cheerful Torah thoughts all of the time, or at least most of the time. Even if you think you are poor at the present time, there is a clear-cut path to wealth, prescribed by *Pirkei Avos,* which you can apply immediately:

Whoever fulfills the Torah in poverty will merit to fulfill it eventually in wealth.
(*Avos* 4:11)

This is based upon Hashem's system, "In the way a person is determined to go, he will be led" (*Makos* 10b).

One who utilizes his free will properly to serve Hashem will be granted more opportunities to do so. Hashem will give him more wealth to enable him to devote more time to Torah and mitzvos.

"If there is no Torah, there is no sustenance. If there is no sustenance, there is no Torah" (*Avos* 3:21). Money is not edible, but, if used in the right way, it can serve as a vehicle to enable a person to learn more Torah.

If you need to purchase an expensive item or pay a large bill which seems beyond your means, do not think, *I just can't afford it*. If you do so, your brain will stop working on the issue and you will refrain from praying to Hashem for help in the matter. Instead, ask yourself, *How can I come up with this money with Hashem's help?* This will enable you to think of ideas that will help and push you to daven more.

The power of our thoughts is enormous. We develop our desire and determination by the way we think, speak, and act.

Lesson Six

Positive Thoughts

When you change your thoughts from "I can't do anything" to "I can, with Hashem's help," you will begin to notice how much Hashem helps you with your finances.

Many of life's daily problems are caused by a need or perceived need for money. It occupies people's thoughts to the point where it interferes, at times, with their service to Hashem and their fulfillment of the mitzvos of the mind, such as faith (*emunah*) and trust (*bitachon*) in Hashem. For this reason, it is essential to train oneself to think positive Torah thoughts about money.

> *The more property, the more worry....*
> *The more Torah, the more life.*
> (*Avos* 2:8)

To reap the benefits of this *mishnah*, we must strive to make these lessons a part of our lives. Every negative, harmful, and unproductive thought about money can be removed from our minds and replaced.

If you are anxious over paying your debts, remind yourself, "Paying one's debts is a mitzvah" (*Kesubos* 86a). It is also written that failure to pay one's debts is one of the worst character flaws, from which a person must distance himself (*Avos* 2:14). There are ways to pay off one's debts step by step, and Hashem will help you when you focus on your responsibility.

If you do not know how you will pay for your children's tuition, think of the great mitzvah you are fulfilling by paying those who teach your children Torah. The Gemara teaches that this is one of the things that Hashem provides for you, beyond the amount of money you were granted on Rosh HaShanah for the coming year (*Beitzah* 16a). Thus, there is no reason to worry.

When you keep replacing negative thoughts with phrases from Tanach, Mishnah, and Gemara, you will become stronger and more empowered.

"Who is wealthy?" (*Avos* 4:1). The Mishnah does not answer, "He who has a lot of money." Money can come and go. Rather, it says, "He who is happy with his portion." Learn to appreciate your portion! Your thoughts about money are what make the difference!

Words and Action

Say little and do a lot.
(*Avos* 1:15)

I f you speak about money in a careless, negative way, you may be undermining your future income. "Do not open your mouth to the Satan" (*Berachos* 20a).

Don't say, "I'll never get that job" or "I'll never be rich." Your words serve as a bridge between your thoughts and your actions. When you think of yourself as poor and express negative ideas, you may refrain from taking the actions necessary to achieve wealth. Why push yourself into a self-fulfilling, negative prophecy when you can turn your thoughts into positive ones?

Our Sages spoke positively about wealth, as we see from the following *mishnah*:

The oral tradition is a fence around the Torah,
tithes are a fence around wealth, vows are a fence

around voluntary abstinence, and a fence around wisdom is silence.
(Avos 3:17)

What is the common denominator of these four fences? They all enable us to serve Hashem better.

Saying "I'm broke" sounds negative. Instead, try, "This, too, is for the best" and "I will learn how to improve myself."

"I'll never be rich" — this is against a *mishnah*, *Avos* 4:11 (see Lesson Five, above).

When you repeat words often enough, they will be internalized. You will suffer if you are repeating words that are not Torah truths. Practice saying the positive:

- ❖ "I will pay off all of my debts, with Hashem's help."

- ❖ "I will work energetically so that I get a raise and meet my obligations."

- ❖ "I will save up enough money to buy...."

- ❖ "I will spend only what I can afford to spend now."

- ❖ "I will save a little from every paycheck in order to fulfill my Torah obligations in the future."

Priorities

*Reduce your involvement in business and involve
yourself in Torah.*
(*Avos* 4:12)

With this statement, the Mishnah is teaching us that we must not confuse our priorities in life. We need to reduce material clutter and numerous work obligations in order to achieve success in Torah.

Make giving *ma'aser* (a tenth of your earnings to charity) a priority. When we do this, we are actually benefitting ourselves, because *tzedakah* is an eternal investment plan. The rewards remain forever.

Next, cut back on how you spend the money that you take home. When we save money, we are also saving time, because every dollar we spend will take time to earn back. Prioritize and spend only on what is really necessary.

The general purpose of having money is to have

the ability to learn Torah and fulfill mitzvos. Thus, the main priority is to focus on one's Torah and mitzvah goals. "All those who accept upon themselves the yoke of Torah will be relieved from the yoke of the government and the yoke of earning a livelihood" (*Avos* 3:6).

Hashem is offering to work with us. It is as if He is saying, "You choose the way you desire to lead your life, and I will enable you to do it even better."

Sometimes we get caught up in the material world and begin cluttering our lives with more and more objects — furniture, toys, luxuries, and clothing that we don't really need. Strive to avoid and eliminate these unnecessary purchases. They only cost money and take up space, and they may never be used!

Why do we tend to keep useless items around? We think we may need them. But the truth is that they just prevent us from focusing on our priorities. Surrounded by clutter, we have trouble finding what we need, and we often don't see what we have and don't appreciate it. "Who is wealthy? He who is happy with his portion" (*Avos* 4:1) — not one who keeps buying and storing.

Clutter is not limited to the physical. Clutter in your mind prevents you from focusing on Torah thoughts, such as reflecting on all the good that you are granted from Hashem. Clutter and lack of organization robs you of your capacity to develop your full potential.

Reduce the clutter, and you can clear the way to more Torah, energy, and achievement.

When you seem to be pushed around by all of your activities and endeavors, when you don't have time to think about yourself and what you are doing — it is time to slow down and tell yourself: "Obviously, Hashem, who is the Master Teacher, is trying to teach me something. Perhaps He is saying, 'Wake up, there is something urgent you must learn. What are you living for? What is the purpose of all this running? Do you think that you are chasing your livelihood? You may be running in the wrong direction.' "

Do you really want to be so busy, or do you want to do the right things in the most efficient way?

Proper Use of Wealth

Tithes [ma'asros] are a fence around wealth.
(*Avos* 3:17)

This *mishnah* is explained by Rabbi Shamshon Rafael Hirsch as a lesson in utilizing wealth properly. There are three types of *ma'aser* in the Torah. Each one enables us to keep our priorities straight and implement our life goals.

The first *ma'aser* (*ma'aser rishon*), which was given to the *Levi'im* (the teachers of the Jewish people in the time of the Beis HaMikdash), teaches us to attend to our spiritual needs and support our Torah teachers before gratifying our physical needs. We all need mentors. As the Mishnah teaches, one must acquire a teacher for himself (*Avos* 1:6) — it is most essential for our success in life. We tend to lose sight of our goals, focusing on money or honor instead of on achieving more of our potential and learning more. We need a rebbe to open our eyes to Hashem's plan for our growth.

The second *ma'aser* (*ma'aser sheini*), which we must eat in the Holy City, Yerushalayim, teaches us that even mundane activities such as eating can become mitzvos. In addition, we learn that we should place ourselves in the right environment so that we can serve Hashem better.

The third *ma'aser* (*ma'aser ani*), which was given to the poor, teaches us that a portion of our possessions are to be shared with others. Hashem provides us with money so that we can serve as His agents and provide for those who are not as well off.

Your money should provide you with spiritual and material benefits. In addition to providing for yourself and your family, it enables you to emulate Hashem by giving to others. Remember, though, that money can pull you down if you don't put up fences to protect yourself.

Three Foundations

*The world stands upon three things: Torah,
avodah [service of Hashem], and acts of
kindness.*
(*Avos* 1:2)

We have to make this *mishnah* the focus of our
lives. It is our job to make the world a more perfect place, permeated with Torah, *avodah*, and kindness. We can help create a truly happy world if we
develop ourselves in these three areas.

Money can enable us to accomplish these goals.
But there is a great problem that comes with making
money: We begin to think that it is great to own expensive things and be wealthy. In addition to thinking things like *I must be someone special* and *I am so
powerful*, we become selfish and even greedy. We
want more and more.

We must put a stop to it. Put your foot down
firmly and declare to yourself, "I am not going to be
distracted from my true goals:

❖ "Torah — my guiding force which helps me achieve closeness to Hashem and fulfill the mitzvos,

❖ "*Avodah* — serving Hashem with prayer and gratitude, and

❖ "*Chesed* — being a giver."

Besides the ten percent of your earnings that you always give to charity, you can make your business or job into a place of *chesed*. Whether you are a teacher, doctor, nurse, secretary, repairman, computer programmer, or businessman, you can make it your business to go out of your way to help people. Even if you have no money, you can train yourself to be a "giver" by giving whatever you can to whomever you can regularly.

Never work to merely make money. Work to serve Hashem and utilize money to serve Hashem more. Money should work for you, allowing you to progress in achieving your goals in life.

Part III

Business Lessons

Introduction

The business lessons in this portion of the book can be applied to all forms of business endeavors, including giving *tzedakah* and doing *chesed* with others. As we will see, they come from *Pirkei Avos*, which contains the lessons of the Torah that govern and direct us to success in all areas of life.

We are all in one type of business or another. Even mitzvos such as *tzedakah* or *hachnasas orchim*, which are dependent upon another person as a recipient, can be viewed as a business. When we involve ourselves in these mitzvos, for example by inviting people to our homes for Shabbos, we have to pay attention to every detail — not only the food, but also the needs, wishes, and feelings of our guests — so that we can be successful in this "business." If we do not do the mitzvah correctly, we may not be able to get "repeat business." This means that even though all the ingredients in the food were absolutely kosher, another important ingredient, *chesed*, was lacking.

It is the same with all business endeavors. In order to really succeed in building our business, increasing our clientele, and making more money, we need to always keep in mind that we will only succeed if we follow the Torah's guidelines for success, and that what we are actually doing is a *chesed* for other people.

Wide Open

Let your house be wide open.
(*Avos* 1:5)

Abasic Torah principle for helping others is to make yourself accessible to them. Not only should this be a foundation of your home, but it should also be a cornerstone of your business. Consider: Are you missing customers in your immediate surroundings just because you have never reached out to them?

You have to promote your product in a unique way in order to reach out to more people. However, when you succeed in finding a dynamic promotional idea, it should not lead you to arrogance because that will only harm your business prospects.

Never overlook the opportunities hiding in front of your face. Shlomo HaMelech teaches us, "Wisdom is before an understanding person, but a fool looks to the ends of the earth" (*Mishlei* 17:24).

Hashem created us with the capacity to be creative and promote our ideas, and thereby serve Him and others. Utilize what He has given you to improve your business! A business can multiply its customers greatly by being "wide open," making itself available to others. Even by concentrating on all the people on your block and your neighborhood, you can expand greatly.

How about inviting the people who surround you to your home or business for a "say hello" event? Offer them something to eat and drink, as Avraham Avinu did, and perhaps even give them something to take home. Your best potential customers are all around you, but you may be too closed up to notice them.

Every person has many connections, many spheres of influence all around. Do the people around you all know what you do and how well you do it? Do you have a good method to inform them? Avraham Avinu designed four doors to his home, one on each side, so that he would not miss any potential "customers" who might pass by. This idea has been followed by major department stores, which have doors on all sides to attract as many customers as possible. Do you make it easy for your customers to find you? Do you make them feel welcome? Is your sincerity in truly being open for their business apparent?

If something you worked on needs some adjustment or someone orders something that is out of stock, how eager are you to go out of your way to help your client? Realize that *chesed* does not mean to give people what you want to give them, but, rather, to give them what they need. This is the secret to an open home and an open business.

Be Sincere

Greet every person with a pleasant, cheerful face.
(*Avos* 1:15)

Show that you care about your customers or clients. This extends beyond the greeting — think about what will make them happier, and act on it.

Do you ever contact your customers just to share an idea or to offer them a lead that will help them? Always show people that you appreciate them in general and that you look out for their interests in specific ways. Offer them items of interest that demonstrate your positive feelings toward them.

Always provide your customers with a bonus, more than what they pay for — "Say little and do a lot" (*Avos* 1:15).

Is there any reason that a business should not have drinks and a bowl of fresh fruit handy to offer its clients? People feel special when you think about them and their needs. Often they will frequent certain stores just because of minor differences in service, such as a more comfortable environment, more perks, or even the availability of a clean bathroom.

Ask yourself: "How can we provide our customers with better service?"

Ask others the same question. Ask your customers, too. Are you doing more for your customers than your competition does? Why not?

When you ask your customers what they need, want, or appreciate, you are showing them how important they are to you.

Even when you have to be businesslike and request payment, you can do it pleasantly. There is a difference between saying, "You'd better pay your bill as soon as you can," and saying, "Your prompt payment is greatly appreciated." When you speak pleasantly, people will be much more likely to do as you ask.

It is essential not to be prejudiced against potential customers. You have to speak to every single person that you come across in a positive way. Invest your energy, with passion, into your work, so that it is obvious that you believe in what you do.

Besides the obvious business value, a Jew always has to be aware of the impression he makes because every situation can lead to a tremendous *kiddush Hashem* (a sanctification of Hashem's Name).

Promote Your Message

*One who promotes his name loses it; one who
does not increase [his Torah learning]
decreases it.*
(*Avos* 1:13)

This was one of Hillel's famous sayings. Don't tell
people how good you are — why should they be
interested in hearing about it? Don't toot your own
horn; instead, show that you are there to serve your
customers.

People will remember you more if you demonstrate that you care about them. If, when you say
hello to someone, you ask his name, where he comes
from, what he does, and how you can be helpful to
him, chances are he will become interested in you,
too. But remember that your goal is to help people,
as Avraham Avinu did. He offered people lavish
meals and then taught them about Hashem. This is
what Hashem wants from us — to help others in
whatever you specialize in.

Do people enjoy speaking to you? If not, how do you expect to develop positive connections and relationships? Do you greet people warmly, or do you tend to ignore them? There are three *mishnayos* in *Avos* that we need to remember every time we meet a person:

❖ "Greet every person with a pleasant, cheerful face" (*Avos* 1:15).

❖ "Be first to greet every person" (ibid. 4:20).

❖ "Greet every person with joy" (ibid. 3:16).

We learn from these three teachings that it is a mitzvah to express excitement and enthusiasm when we greet other people. When you shake hands, for example, is it with warm enthusiasm? Is your voice modulated to make the other person feel happy? Do you say, "I'm glad to meet you"? Do you speak about a subject of interest to the other person?

Try smiling and asking a thoughtful question, such as, "Which part of this week's parashah or today's *daf* did you find most exciting?" You will be surprised at the positive reaction you may get. Many "ordinary" *frum* Jews have very interesting personal insights or lessons they have heard from others that they will gladly share with you — if you ask. You are doing them a great favor, because at times they may feel, *Who would want to hear a vort from me?* A wise person is eager to learn from every person (see *Avos*

4:1), and the rewards are many.

The Gemara (*Berachos* 23a) teaches that to create a positive, pleasant, and memorable encounter, one should share a Torah insight. This is an excellent way of making yourself worth remembering.

When you go out of your way to always be friendly to others, when you meet and greet others with joy, you fulfill the mitzvah of loving your fellow man as yourself (see *Vayikra* 19:18). You also gain a fringe benefit of being remembered favorably, which can lead to increased business opportunities — which are actually more opportunities for you to perform *chesed*.

Six Super Seconds

As we mentioned in the previous lesson, every time you meet someone you have a perfect opportunity to fulfill the *mishnayos* in *Avos* on greeting others cheerfully and showing an interest in them.

If you want to go beyond these basic requirements, you can endeavor to get people to think. For example, in response to "How are you?" try saying, "*Baruch Hashem*, I'm breathing, my heart is pumping blood, and my kidneys are functioning!"

A meaningful and intriguing response will usually illicit a request for more information or the comment, "That is a great point!" Don't give surface answers. Your customers will be more interested and willing to give you their business if they feel you are special.

In addition, you can teach others in many subtle ways, through signs or posters on your office wall. Perhaps you can make others aware of the six constant mitzvos — the ones we are obligated to fulfill at all times. The six mitzvos are:

1. Believe that Hashem created and controls all.

2. There is none but Him.

3. He is One.

4. Love Him.

5. Fear Him.

6. Avoid temptation.

Every time we interact with other people, we have an opportunity to make a difference in their lives. Even in your business you can try to enlighten people. Sometimes you will see right away that your words hit their mark and the person will never forget the message. You will gain tremendously, and so will they.

On the other hand, not everyone will be receptive to your message if you don't keep an open mind. Deal with each person in the way that will work for him.

Lesson Five

Loving Others

*Be of the students of Aharon, loving peace and
pursuing peace, loving people....*
(*Avos* 1:12)

Although we are cautioned to avoid excessive talk
(see *Avos* 1:17), there are times where it is a
mitzvah to schmooze with others. It is important to
develop a positive connection with others by means
of an enjoyable, friendly atmosphere. People will enjoy your company if you are positive, dynamic, or
funny. If you compliment people and offer to help
them, they will see that you care about them.

The Mishnah teaches us to love our work (*Avos*
1:10). One of the side benefits that we gain from an
up-beat attitude about our work is that our customers will gravitate to us and be motivated to do more
business with us. It's good customer service to like
your customers, and the results are exceptional
when it comes to sales. Always try to make the inter-
action between yourself and your customer unpres-

sured and pleasant. In this way, you are fulfilling the command to love peace and to love people.

Along the same lines, we are taught to avoid the negative:

> *Do not be scornful of any person.*
> (*Avos* 4:3)

Never write off a customer because he dresses improperly, seems uninformed, or in general makes a bad impression.

Helping and loving others is one of the greatest mitzvos of the Torah. The more you care about others, the more you are serving Hashem, who desires that you be kind and loyal when serving others.

Learning from Others

Who is wise? He who learns from every person.
(*Avos* 4:1)

Make a list of every boss you ever had and study each of them, thinking of what you can learn from him or her. You will see that you can learn something valuable from each one — whether it is something positive you picked up or something negative you decided to stay away from. Think to yourself, *How can I emulate that action* or *How can I improve on that?*

It is not up to you to complete all of the work, but you are also not free to exempt yourself from it.
(*Avos* 2:21)

It has been said that the best way to get a free higher education is to ask questions of people who have succeeded in whatever field they are in and enjoy what they are doing. We are surrounded by such people all the time. These people can answer such questions as, "What helped you achieve success in your field of endeavor?" and "How did you build up your company?"

The lessons you learn will benefit you in many ways. You will also be amazed to discover how many insights can be applied to your own life. There are fantastic opportunities available — if you are alert enough to grab them. Every single day of life and every person you encounter is a learning experience. Prepare some questions that you feel comfortable with and use them often.

Keep in mind also that the group of people from whom you can learn (that is, everyone) includes your customers. Every customer who criticizes you or complains about your work is someone you can learn from, when you realize that Hashem has sent him or her to teach you some valuable lesson.

If someone wants to return an item because of a reasonable complaint, pay his refund gladly. Consider this a type of "tuition" for learning valuable lessons about your merchandise. You can improve your business greatly if you listen to the customer's reason for returning the item and make improvements on that basis.

Lesson Seven

Say a Little

Say little and do a lot.
(*Avos* 1:15)

We should never forget how important silence is. "I have found nothing better for a body than silence" (*Avos* 1:17). One of the benefits of silence is that it enables us to think more about the words we say and only speak after careful consideration.

It is important to put emphasis on certain words. For example, try to use a person's first name. This is one of the greatest forms of kindness, because every person's favorite word is his own name. If you have trouble remembering names, practice it in advance.

It is actually also a form of emulating Hashem to say a person's name, since we see that Hashem refers to people by name in the Torah (see, for example, *Bereishis* 22:1).

In addition to choosing your words carefully, it is also helpful to write down your goals. If you tend to talk a lot about what you plan to do but then never seem to accomplish half of it, this may help you greatly. Writing will force you to be more specific about your goals and help you clarify what you really want to do. It will also help you become more committed to achieving your goals. "Saying little" in a concrete way will lead to "doing a lot," with the help of Hashem.

Saying, "I would like to improve my customer service" or "I think my product can be marketed better" is not going to accomplish much. Nothing will happen unless you sit down and plan exactly what you can do, investing time, effort, and prayer. Only "say a little" because talk alone is cheap and misleading.

Included in "saying little" is the idea that the words you say should be invested with the right feelings. Put emotional energy into your words. What you say will then carry more weight. The more emotional energy you put into your words, the more your audience will be compelled to listen and accept your message.

Who to Blame

If I am not for myself, who will be for me?
(*Avos* 1:14)

It often feels good to have someone to blame for our failings. But that is not a Torah approach. For long-term success, we must memorize and apply the above quote from *Avos*.

If your employees or your clients are not meeting your expectations, it is easy to blame them when things go wrong. Rather than blame them, though, think of how you can improve the situation.

Hashem has granted us free will. The *yetzer hara* (evil inclination) is always giving us challenges. But is he controlling your life, or are you?

"There are three ways to know the character of a person: through his pocket, his drinks [i.e., when he is drunk], and his anger" (*Eiruvin* 62b). When a person sees the way you handle your money, he can learn a lot about you — whether you are generous, humble, and happy, or miserly, arrogant, and tense.

How would you like to be viewed? It is your choice. Don't think, *I'll never be able to change.* You are the one in charge.

If you worry too much about your money or you never feel that you have enough, you can focus on the lessons we have quoted from *Avos* and gain peace of mind. For example, "Who is happy? He who is happy with his portion" (*Avos* 4:1). Repeat this lesson over and over to yourself, and your sales and income will begin to look better.

You can make a conscious decision to change your business practices and your attitude toward money. You will only benefit if you do this — don't settle for less, thinking you are not capable of learning new methods or thought patterns.

Develop definite goals and invest your efforts in achieving them. It is essential that you do it — as the Mishnah teaches, "If I am not for myself, who will be for me?"

Cherishing Your Friend's Money

*Your friend's money should be as dear to you as
your own.*
(*Avos* 2:17)

The most basic ingredient in good customer service is to be careful with your customers' money and possessions.

Do you guarantee that the price will not be raised after the job is completed? Is the quality of the work you do always satisfactory? And if not, are you eager to rectify it immediately to avoid transgressing the Torah prohibition against theft? These important principles should be the first rules of your business.

If you focus on the quality and the service you offer, rather than on the price you will charge, you will accelerate your growth tremendously. One of the best-kept secrets in business, easy to remember, but difficult to implement consistently, is: Promise a little, but deliver a lot (based on *Avos* 1:14).

This follows also from the concept of the mitzvah to "love your fellow Jew as yourself" (*Vayikra* 19:18) and from the directive to "love [your] work" (*Avos* 1:10). Why does the Mishnah use such a powerful word — *love* your work, a word that is used in the Torah only in regard to Hashem and people? Work is the vehicle through which we express our love toward Hashem and people. Internalize this by applying it regularly. Your actions always speak louder than your words.

People will quickly pick up on how you feel about them and their money. In order to increase your business, it is important to implement these lessons.

Lesson Ten

Wealth Insurance

Tithes are a fence around wealth.
(*Avos* 3:17)

The Gemara has a similar teaching that applies to all forms of kindness: "The 'salt' [preservation] of money is kindness" (*Kesubos* 66b).

When you give others something of value, you make a positive impression on them. Your promotion does not have to be an expensive ad; even a small gift that you give people goes a long way. If you demonstrate that you care about others, you will succeed in business — and in life.

Train yourself to care about others and do something about demonstrating your care! Every customer is a Heaven-sent opportunity for You to open your heart to others.

Your underlying message should be, "I'm not just trying to make money off you. I like you, and I want to develop an ongoing relationship with you." Giving something to others will bring more returns to you in the long run, but the key is to do it out of *chesed* and caring.

When you give money away, you insure your wealth, because you are thereby training yourself to realize that your money is granted to you by Hashem.

When you give money away, you will break loose from the chains of money controlling your life. You will put your focus on the Source of all money, the Creator of the Universe, the Owner and controller of all finances. Hashem will then reward you measure for measure. You will benefit, and your recipients do, too.

Part IV

The Benefits of
Giving Ma'aser

Introduction

One of the cardinal rules of financial affairs is the following lesson from the Gemara:

> *Give a tenth to charity [ma'aser] so that you will become wealthy.*
> (*Taanis 9a*)

This guarantee is so certain that we can even test Hashem Yisbarach with it. The *gemara* quotes the *navi* who says, "[Hashem says,] 'Bring all the tithes to the storehouse, so that there will be food in My house, and please test Me through this — if I will not open the windows of the sky for you and pour out blessing to you without limit'" (*Malachi* 3:10).

If you set aside ten percent of all that you earn, up front, and give it away to those who need it, Hashem promises, "I will make you wealthy."

This mitzvah is so important that the Rambam (*Hilchos Melachim* 9:1) lists it as one of the first ten mitzvos practiced by our forefathers Avraham,

Yitzchak, and Yaakov.

Why is giving *ma'aser* so important and how does it help us achieve wealth?

By giving a tenth of your earnings to serve Hashem you demonstrate that you understand that the entire amount, including the remaining nine-tenths, is a gift to you from Him.

In addition, by giving *ma'aser* you are training yourself to believe that Hashem has more than enough for all of us. He gives us more than we need for ourselves so that we can give to others, in order to remind us who is in charge. Hashem could give the money directly to those in need, but He chose to do us a favor and allow us to give it to them, providing us with the opportunity to improve ourselves.

We should never feel that giving *ma'aser* is a burden — "I have to give *ma'aser* because that's what it says in the Torah, but I really would prefer to keep the money for myself." Instead, we should realize that giving *ma'aser* is a privilege, and it will cause us to prosper. It is the secret that brings about our prosperity.

Will Hashem always make it obvious that He is rewarding us for giving *ma'aser*?

Hashem is asking us to test Him. This implies that if we do our part, then, with a discerning eye and an understanding heart, we will be able to appreciate His response to us.

However, there can be two exceptions to the promise of wealth:

1. If a person is deficient in other areas, such as in his Torah study, prayer, or Shabbos observance, he should not expect Hashem to make him prosper just because he gives *ma'aser*.

2. If a person does not care for wealth in the material sense, preferring a different form of wealth, such as having many children or authoring many *sefarim*, Hashem may prosper his efforts in those areas.

The quality of one's life does not depend only on how much money he accumulates. You define your life by your attitude and your actions. This is why *ma'aser* is so enriching.

Benefits of Giving

When you give away 10 percent of all your prof-its, you will gain in many ways.

1. The fact that you have what to give away re-minds you to be grateful for what Hashem has granted you.

2. You become a giver, trying to fill other peo-ple's needs, which is the secret of *chesed*. You are becoming more like Hashem and follow-ing His ways, which in itself is making you wealthy.

3. Helping others makes you feel different about who you are. You know you can affect others' lives, and this empowers you to accomplish more in your own life.

4. The financial returns are truly automatic. Keep your eyes open and you will see them. You may receive financing for an income-producing property at a lower interest rate

and save a bundle. You may be offered payment for jobs that you were willing to do without pay. You may get something on sale, at a discount, or as a special deal, all as a result of your giving *ma'aser*.

5. You learn self-control by putting aside some of your earnings. This will also curb some of your desire to earn more. Our Sages teach that if a person has one hundred dollars, he will want two hundred (*Koheles Rabbah* 1:34). If you decrease the amount you have on hand, you will also decrease the amount you want, thus satisfying yourself with less.

Lesson Two

Keep Growing

The concept of *ma'aser* — giving back from what we receive — helps us stay alert and never to take success for granted. We must be grateful to Hashem every day for the income He provides. We can never allow ourselves to become complacent.

People who become too comfortable stop growing spiritually. They stop working as hard to create value in their lives. If you are not actively climbing the ladder toward Hashem, you are sliding away. Every experience in life can be used either as an opportunity for growth or a reason to decline. Every success can be a springboard to greater heights or a chance to massage your ego and become more haughty.

If you remember these lessons when you give *ma'aser*, you will give properly, with gratitude to Hashem for granting you the means to give in the first place. Then you will activate the system of measure-for-measure. You deserve more because you used the previous amounts properly.

If you do your part, you will deserve Hashem's bounty. The Gemara (*Bava Basra* 10a) recommends that a person give charity before he prays. Why? Because when you help others, you too deserve help from Hashem.

Comparison Motivation

.

The envy of scholars increases wisdom.
(Bava Basra 22a)

Comparing oneself to others is a natural tendency. This can be used positively or negatively. If you view yourself as superior, comparisons can lead to pride and arrogance. On the other hand, if you realize that you are less superior, you can motivate yourself to work harder and accomplish more, like your associates.

Giving *ma'aser*, however, is something completely individualized. You give a tenth of what you earn, no matter how much that may be. One who gives ten thousand out of his one hundred thousand is greater in Hashem's eyes than one who gives only half a million when he has earned ten million.

If you want more money, you must ask yourself why. If the answer is "so that I can buy a car as fancy as my neighbor's" or "because I want a vacation to Florida like my boss," then you may not get what you want. But if you want more money to do more mitzvos, then you have a much better chance.

Ask yourself, "Am I doing all I can do with what Hashem has given me up to this point?"

When you dedicate yourself to a project, Hashem will help you succeed. "In the way a person is determined to go, he will be led" (*Makos* 10b).

Similarly, when you distribute your *ma'aser* money properly, Hashem will send you more so that you can continue to give.

Lesson Four

Training Oneself

Every person who has dei'ah [wisdom] will eventually become wealthy.
(Sanhedrin 92a)

Maharsha explains that this *gemara* refers to the understanding that all wealth comes from only one source — the Master of All.

Giving *ma'aser* consciously will help you train yourself to have *dei'ah*. We learn to acknowledge the Source of all wealth, Hashem, who provides everything to everyone, every moment. Hashem wants you to become successful in every area of life — He wants you to thrive with what you have.

We see from Tanach how Hashem provided for Avraham, Yitzchak, Yaakov, Yosef, David, Shlomo, and many others. All of these people were granted wealth as a result of the good they did. When we employ our resources and follow the Torah's guidelines, we too will prosper, with Hashem's help.

Avram was loaded with livestock, silver, and gold.
(*Bereishis* 13:2)

The Torah wants us to know that even though Avraham Avinu became very wealthy, this did not cause an interruption in his service to Hashem. He continued to grow in spirituality and passed many more tests sent his way. In the same way, when we live a life of service to Hashem, He will follow up and prosper our efforts.

If you desire to be a great *ma'aser*-giver, essentially you are devoting yourself to Hashem's service, which is the key to being successful.

Wealth often leads to power and prestige, which a righteous person can use to serve Hashem. What does it take? To always be mindful of Hashem and be humble before Him.

If someone gave you a hundred thousand dollars on condition that 10 percent be given back, would you not energetically fulfill the request?

Give from What You Have

M*a'aser* teaches us not only to give, but also how to give. We are not permitted to give away all of our money because that will prevent us from giving in the future. "One who chooses to give extra should not give more than a fifth, so that he does not become impoverished" (*Kesubos* 50b).

On the other hand, we are not allowed to wait until we become rich before we start giving *ma'aser*. We must give 10 percent of whatever we have right now. Ten percent of ten dollars is one dollar. Start giving now and you will start the process in motion.

We learn from this that whenever we give to others — whether we're giving our time, our money, or anything else — we should not give to the point where we can no longer provide for ourselves. We also should not wait until we have "everything." If someone needs help, give of whatever you have, even if it is just a smile or a listening ear.

Why We Give

Give a tenth to charity so that you will become wealthy.
(*Taanis* 9a)

Although the Gemara teaches that giving *ma'aser* leads to wealth, we should not give only in order to receive back. That would be doing a mitzvah with an ulterior motive, which is referred to as a *"mitzvah shelo lishmah."* Although we are encouraged to do this in the beginning, there is a higher level which we can strive for.

Tosafos explains that the term "so that" (*bishvil*) means to give with the following intent: "I'd like to become wealthy so that I can continue to give more and more. I would like to do good with the money I get. If Hashem does not choose to make me wealthy, I will understand that I may not be worthy. But I will try my best to follow His instructions in order to merit wealth."

There are many benefits that Hashem showers

on those who give *ma'aser* consistently. Hashem is our Shepherd; He cares for us, and we shall not lack (see *Tehillim* 23:1). Giving *ma'aser* is a way to connect to Hashem, who is the source of all prosperity. Understanding this will help us give *ma'aser* sincerely, honestly, with excitement, and with love of Hashem.

When we give with the understanding that Hashem's system will work for us, we are training ourselves in *emunah*. Occasionally we may find ourselves in a financial crunch. This can be solved by correcting our mental attitude and remembering that Hashem is always providing our needs.

Hashem is working with you as your financial partner. When you keep giving a tenth of your earnings to charity because you want a connection to Him (and not because you want money from Him), He will give you whatever you lack.

Unlimited Giving

A person who is generous with his money is extremely praiseworthy. But it is also very important to be generous with physical help, emotional support, and spiritual aid. A warm meal, a kind word, or an inspirational book or tape can change someone's life. (For sample books or tapes, please write to P.O. Box 82, Staten Island, NY, 10309.)

We all have many unique talents which we must learn to recognize and "give *ma'aser*" from. You can brighten the world by offering others a smile, a joke, or a word of encouragement. Hashem, who created the world, empowered us with creativity to be, in a limited sense, like Him. By giving to others with our talents, we are emulating our Creator.

When you give *ma'aser*, you expand your awareness of these principles.

Giving Is Living

When you give *ma'aser*, you are making a statement to Hashem and to people: You are saying that you care about others who are not as fortunate as you are. You are sharing what Hashem has given you, reminding yourself that *chesed* is the foundation of this world.

It is essential to give with love. *Ahavas chesed* (a love for kindness) shows that you are happy and eager to give.

The key to succeeding in this world is to make yourself "indispensable" to Hashem. Although this is actually impossible because Hashem does not need anything or anyone, nevertheless He allows us to serve Him and aid His creations. When we give *ma'aser*, thereby helping others, Hashem will look favorably upon us and help us.

It takes years of persistence, determination, discipline, and enthusiasm to build ourselves up to a high level, but it starts with reaching out to others right now. The possibilities are endless. The more you help others, the more spiritually wealthy you will become. When you dedicate yourself to others, you will find that you yourself are provided with the capabilities to overcome the challenges and adversity in your life.

What do you do when you have financial setbacks despite the amounts of *tzedakah* that you give? Realize that the ups and downs of life occur to teach us lessons — each time something new. We learn to be creative, flexible, and positive even in the face of adversity. The higher you set your heights, the greater you can become.

As a person develops a passion for learning and giving, he will grow and change even when things don't go so well. It is important to have mentors, role models, and others who challenge you to grow. We also need friends and associates to share good and bad times with.

Persistent and relentless pursuit of your goals will grant you special Heavenly assistance that will get you where you want to go. Explore all of the possibilities and opportunities that Hashem sends your way. Doors will open, sometimes unexpectedly, to lead you to your destination.

Setbacks are part of Hashem's program to teach us humility, fortitude, and patience. We have to focus on our faith in Hashem that things will work out

for the best. When we do our best to make a difference for ourselves and others, Hashem helps us grow
and thrive.

Part V

The Alef-Beis of Making Money the Torah Way

Introduction

The world stands on three things: Torah, avodah
[service of Hashem], and acts of kindness.
(*Avos* 1:2)

We know that our job in this world is to uphold
these three pillars of the world. But we also need
to support ourselves and our families. Not infre-
quently, the thought crosses our minds: *How can I
earn more money?*

Here are the Torah basics, facts that will help
you focus on how to increase your business and
earning potential the right way. It is crucial to learn
these Torah guidelines and to refer to them regularly
until they become your automatic response to your
job and your challenges in life.

Even if you are already a successful entrepreneur,
these tips can guide you to your next step. Every move
you make can lead to either more success or failure.

We have organized this work according to the
alef-beis for quick learning and easy reference.

אמונה

Emunah

Everything is in the hands of Hashem. He runs the world, He runs the economy, and He runs your business.

When the Talmud (*Niddah* 70a) teaches how to become wealthy, it says, "Pray for mercy from the Owner of all wealth, as it says, 'Silver and gold are Mine' (*Chaggai* 2:8)."

A person can never touch that which is prepared
for another.
(Yoma 38b)

Ask yourself daily:

❖ Who is really in control?

❖ Who is the real owner of this business?

Fortunate is the person who is constantly afraid.
(*Mishlei* 28:14)

We have to be concerned that we are doing things in the right way. Be sure that your hands are clean from touching that which is not yours, and be careful with other people's money. This is easy when you remember that Hashem is the Source of all wealth.

בטחון
Bitachon

As you internalize the principles of *emunah*, you can also develop your *bitachon*. The actions that you take should be guided by your trust in Hashem, which is founded on your belief.

A note of caution: Hashem wants you to be involved in *hishtadlus* (efforts) on your own behalf, in addition to praying and hoping to Him. Hillel spells this out in his famous teaching: "If I am not for myself, who will be for me?" (*Avos* 1:14).

Another important aspect of *bitachon* is *bench*ing properly, thanking Hashem with heartfelt

appreciation for the abundant sustenance He provides. When we do this, Hashem will provide for us
in a dignified manner (*Sefer HaChinuch* 428).

Whatever you do for a living — no matter who
signs your paycheck — your ultimate Employer is
Hashem. When you realize that you are in Hashem's
employ, you will never be out of work. Hashem is
able and ready to provide you with all of your needs.

Ask yourself daily:

❖ Have I thanked Hashem for my last paycheck?

❖ Am I doing enough *hishtadlus*?

גמילות חסדים
Acts of Kindness

If you view your work as *chesed*, you will have more drive and enthusiasm. Try to provide what people need, offering them quality work or merchandise.

Do market research. Ask people what type of products they need or want. Once you have identified the needs of others, try to satisfy those needs.

Do you work with joy, energy, and purpose? Do you focus on how you can help people with your talents and thus improve the world in some way? Which of your innate talents could you cultivate more in order to assist a greater number of people?

Ask yourself daily:

❖ How can I help others more?

❖ How can I make people feel good about themselves?

❖ What valuable product or service can I give the next customer I serve?

דעת

Wisdom

Every person who has dei'ah [wisdom] will eventually become wealthy.
(Sanhedrin 92a)

In addition to keeping in mind the facts that Hashem is in control and all wealth is from Him, we must use our intellect and our potential in order to become wealthy.

Do you realize that you were created by Hashem with a unique personality and unique skills, talents, and experiences? Do not allow yourself to think that you are average. There is no such thing.

Why are you alive? Certainly it is not merely to make money. You are much greater than that. The quality of your work is dependent on how much of your *neshamah*'s inner power you utilize. You can achieve personal greatness and growth by means of your work. Use understanding and knowledge, Hashem's gifts to you, and you will discover that spiritual and material wealth is the natural result.

If you stick to your niche,
you will become rich.

הודאה

Thanking

If you do not thank Hashem for all that He has given you in the past and all that He continues to give you constantly, why should He give you more?

Even when we have troubles — financial or otherwise — we should thank Hashem.

You will say on that day: "I thank You, Hashem, for You were angry at me."
(Yeshayah 12:1)

Imagine someday thanking Hashem for your troubles. Indeed, this will be the case. When troubles come our way, they may actually be for our salvation. Hashem's plans are beyond our comprehension, but He is always in control of all the events and affairs of the individual and of the world.

Even if you lose your job, you can thank Hashem. Perhaps He is hinting to you that you are much greater than that job and He has other, better opportunities for you.

All that the Merciful One does is for the good.
(*Berachos* 60b)

ותרנות

Being Generous

Giving generously of your money to *tzedakah* and to other forms of helping others is a good practice.

Materialistic people often find it difficult to part with their money. The Torah requires us to be different. A Torah Jew desires money only for the purpose of doing mitzvos and serving Hashem.

One of the questions that you have to keep asking yourself is, Why do I want money? What is it worth? As long as you are generous with your money for mitzvos, you can guage your motives for making money.

זהירות

Being Careful

All of a person's sustenance [i.e., income] is de-cided for him on Rosh HaShanah [and therefore he should be careful not to spend extravagantly — Rashi].
(Beitzah 15a)

One should have a budget and be careful not to spend beyond his means. However, the *gemara* continues that three areas of expenditure are excluded from the amount fixed on Rosh HaShanah: those of Shabbos, *yom tov*, and children's education. These three things are outside of your regular budget from Heaven.

One who checks on his properties daily will save money.
(*Chullin* 105a)

When Yaakov Avinu was very wealthy and owned many servants, he retraced his steps to pick up some small containers he had left behind (*Bereishis* 32:25). This teaches how careful one must be with his possessions, realizing that he is responsible for the property Hashem "loans" him.

Another example of this is when Moshe's parents placed him in a reed basket in the Nile River to save his life (see *Shemos* 2:3). Why did they use such a cheap type of basket? One answer given by the Gemara (*Sotah* 12a) is that the righteous cherish their honestly earned income and do not waste money on something expensive when a cheaper item will suffice.

In both of these cases, the Gemara teaches that one should be careful not to waste his money.

חיזוק

Strengthening

Four activities require constant strengthening: To-rah, good deeds, prayer, and earning a livelihood.
(Berachos 32b)

Rashi explains that one always has to strength-en himself with all his power in order to do his job correctly. Making a living is grouped together with three obvious mitzvos because money is the fuel nec-essary to keep everything going.

The Rambam teaches, "A person is obligated to work with all his strength, as Yaakov the Righteous said, 'With all my strength I worked for your father'

(*Bereishis* 31:6). Therefore he received reward even in this world, as it says, 'And the man increased exceedingly' (ibid. 30:43)" (*Hilchos Sechirus* 17:7).

טוב

Good

Two are better than one.
(*Koheles* 4:9)

Every person who wants to succeed in life needs to be actively involved with others.

Are you a visionary? A good manager? A top salesman? A skilled organizer? Be aware of your strengths and realistic about your limitations, and find partners or employees who can provide what you lack.

Every morning, we thank Hashem for "providing me with all of my needs." Keep in mind that

Hashem also provides us with able assistants. Every person we interact with has come in contact with us for our benefit.

יפה

Pleasant

There are eight things that are difficult in a large quantity but pleasant [yaffeh] in a small quantity...an occupation, wealth....
(Gittin 70a)

How can too much prosperity be a negative thing? Rashi explains that the *gemara* refers to wealth that distracts one from Torah study and causes him to become arrogant. When a person is blessed with wealth, he must be careful not to let it ruin him.

"He made everything pleasant in its right time"
(Koheles 3:11). This teaches that Hashem makes
each person's occupation pleasant to him.
(Berachos 43b)

Hashem causes each person to like a certain type of job. Everyone's calling is unique.

If you do not enjoy your job, make every effort to find out your particular calling and try to involve yourself in work suited to you. Do not resign yourself to a life without personal meaning. Ask yourself, "If I had three months left to live, what would I focus on in my life?"

Pirkei Avos exhorts us to "love work" (*Avos* 1:10) because work is such a fundamental part of life. You were created to do a certain type of work which serves to express your unique talents and abilities. With Hashem's help, you will be able to find your niche.

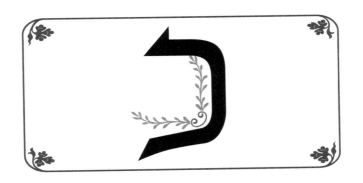

כל

All

All your deeds should be for the sake of Heaven.
(*Avos* 2:17)

It is a mitzvah to provide for yourself and your family and to support your Torah study and that of your family. In addition, your actual occupation may be a kindness to others.

The mitzvos you can do while working are endless. All you need to do is focus on them.

(It should be noted that we are not discussing here the issue of *kollel* for one who is capable of devoting himself to full-time learning. That is a super ideal which requires a whole book of its own.)

לעולם

Always

A person should always...divide his property into three parts: one third in real estate, one third in merchandise, and one third in liquid assets [in order to be able to benefit from sudden opportunities — Rashi].
(Bava Metzia 42a)

Ask yourself:

❖ Is my portfolio diversified as our Sages teach?

❖ Do I keep some cash on hand so as not to waste money by charging things?

מעשר

Ma'aser

Give a tenth [of your money] to charity so that you will become wealthy.
(Taanis 9a)

People are often afraid to give away large amounts of money to *tzedakah. What if I suddenly lose my job or suffer losses in business?* they wonder. *How can I give away money I may someday need myself?*

It is crucial to realize that Hashem provides everything we need, at all times. The more we give, showing our care for others, the more He will give us, showing His care for us.

נטילת ידים

Washing Your Hands

*One who washes with a lot of water will be
blessed with a lot of money.*
(*Shabbos* 62b)

This lesson is taught by Rabbi Chisda who became so exceedingly wealthy that the Gemara
(*Moed Katan* 28a) teaches that other Sages would
pray to be as wealthy as him.

Washing your hands with a lot of water demonstrates your desire to perform mitzvos in the best way
possible. Furthermore, clean hands are a symbol of integrity and of investing your full efforts in an endeavor.

סבלנות

Patience

*Patience is worth four hundred zuz
[i.e., a large sum of money].*
(Berachos 20a)

One of the most important keys to success is patience. If you launch a business prematurely, before understanding all the factors that are involved, you may run up many debts that could have been avoided by taking things slowly.

You need patience, perspective, perseverance, and, above all, prayer.

One who pushes against time will not succeed.
One who yields to time will succeed.
(*Eiruvin* 13b)

Rashi explains: One who does his utmost to become wealthy, even traveling to distant places to push for his success when things do not seem to go well, will not succeed. However, one who is patient and relaxed will eventually be successful with time. One reason for this is that Hashem is teaching the person that wealth is not determined solely by the efforts we put in. Hashem bestows wealth according to His schedule.

עושר

Wealth

Who is wealthy? He who is happy with his portion.
(Avos 4:1)

Count your blessings, and you will soon see how wealthy you are.

(You may have to take a day off to do this accounting, but it will be worth it. You will begin to achieve true wealth!)

Perhaps this is included in the secret behind the Gemara's teaching, "Honor your wife and you will become wealthy" (*Bava Metzia* 59a).

Your wife and children are gifts to you from Hashem. When you treat them with respect, Hashem will treat you with respect as well. Your income is determined by your behavior at home, which is observed by Hashem just as much as your behavior at work.

פרנסה

Livelihood

Three keys are in Hashem's hands and not given to an emissary: The key of rains [i.e., livelihood], the key of life, and the key of resurrection of the dead.
(*Taanis 2a*)

No matter what happens to us, we must remember that our livelihood is in Hashem's hands.

When we wake up in the morning, we have to thank Hashem for what He has given us, because we never know what the coming day will bring. Before the sun sets, our lives may change in an instant.

Whether it be a chance meeting, an unexpected job offer, or an abrupt dismissal, realize that Hashem is guiding you and testing you. When you have to make a choice between job security or Torah values, realize that security is an illusion. Hashem is the sustainer. With His help, we can overcome any challenge. There is no such thing as "making money," only "meriting money."

Ask yourself:

❖ What does Hashem really want from me?

❖ Which job is right for me, for my personal and professional growth?

צדקה

Charity

Charity saves from death.
(Mishlei 10:2)

When you help sustain and provide life for others, Hashem reciprocates with life to you as well.

Occasionally we may wonder why life is so difficult, why so many troubles are coming our way. The answer is that every situation in life is a learning experience, a wake-up call from Hashem.

Despite, or because of, your troubles, you should keep learning about yourself, even if it means realizing there are some things you cannot do. You learn to adjust and grow in many ways.

קדושה

Holiness

If a person sanctifies himself a little, they [i.e., the Heavenly powers] sanctify him greatly. [If he does] below, they sanctify him above. [If he sanctifies himself] in this world, they sanctify him for the World to Come.

(Yoma 39a)

This *gemara* teaches us that we just have to make a bit of effort, and we are then given assistance from Heaven. We can apply this principle to the efforts we make to earn a living — a person should never think that his time and labor are yield-

ing his income. On the contrary, our income is de-
cided on Rosh HaShanah (see *Beitzah* 15a) based on
our deeds. All we have to do is put in some effort,
and the rest will come.

ראש ועושר

Poverty and Wealth

Poverty and wealth do not give me.
(Mishlei 30:8)

This is one of the two prayers that Shlomo HaMelech would always say (ibid., 7).

He is teaching us that rather than seeking out wealth, a person should strive for a middle income. This way he will not suffer from privation nor become haughty.

One who does not have enough money to pay his bills may suffer from financial pressure, whereas one who has more than enough money is challenged to remember that it all comes from Hashem. Both are being tested by Hashem and both need to rise to the challenge and make the best of it.

Both must understand that "the blessing of Hashem is what [really] makes a person wealthy" (*Mishlei* 10:22).

שבת

Shabbos

How does one merit wealth? The Gemara (*Shabbos* 119a) explains that through honoring Shabbos one can earn riches.

Every Shabbos we are reminded that our work all week long is not the end goal in life. Although working for a livelihood is mandated by Hashem, we must maintain the proper perspective. Hashem is the Creator, and the purpose of our lives is to serve Him. By honoring Shabbos, we demonstrate our belief in Hashem and our loyalty to His mitzvos.

The Gemara illustrates this point by relating a

story of a butcher who set aside every nice piece of meat for Shabbos. As a result, he became incredibly wealthy.

תורה

Torah

Another teaching in *Shabbos* (119a) is that one who honors the Torah will merit wealth.

Torah is our guide to life, the book of Hashem's instructions to us. When we treat Hashem's words with the proper respect, Hashem will reward us, in both this world and the next.

SECRETS OF BEING...

Rabbi Moshe Goldberger offers six wonderfully straightforward books that teach us how to take charge of our lives, our choices, and our destinies.

In his inimitable succinct style, Rabbi Goldberger gives us a wealth of ideas culled from the vast storehouse of Jewish wisdom throughout the ages. Brimming with practical advice, unusual insights, and unforgettable words of inspiration, these are small books that contain huge concepts.

TARGUM PRESS Books